Dare
to be
Free

Mission: To Proclaim Transformation and Truth
Publisher: Transformed Publishing, Cocoa, FL
Website: www.transformedpublishing.com
Email: transformedpublishing@gmail.com

ISBN: 978-1-953241-73-3

Dare to be Free

From Loneliness to Empowerment

Available in English and Spanish

Julia Manriquez

Dedication

I dedicate this book to the many women I met along the way, who shared their testimonies with me and to whom I am eternally grateful. But, most especially, someone who is no longer with us and who gave his life for what he believed to be his love. May God have you by His side.

Table of Contents

Introduction

From the moment the Bible mentioned woman was created from man's rib some men have wrongly believed themselves to be the owner of her. Throughout history, and in our society, many women have been demeaned, denigrated and received little recognition for their true abilities and undeniable virtues. Perhaps this is what frightens some men, who, in their attempt to control women, resort to force and oppression.

In some cultures, women do not even own the fruit of their wombs, with no participation in most important decisions or positions. Their role is limited to household chores, and they are often forced to marry against their will.

In certain societies, women do not have the right to have an opinion and must walk several meters behind men. They are forced to wear shoes that deform their feet and to obey their husbands in everything.

Psychological and verbal abuse are manifestations of this long history of oppression. This type of abuse leaves no visible marks, but its effects are devastating. Women who suffer psychological and verbal abuse face constant contempt, manipulation and control that undermine their self-esteem and sense of identity. It is an insidious form of violence that, although invisible, is deeply destructive.

I write this book because I feel I owe it to women who are living, or have lived, the terrible experience of verbal, psychological, physical, economic, and sexual abuse. I do it because I, myself, experienced two cruel and difficult to forget abuses: verbal and psychological. I managed to escape from those tangled networks, now finding purpose in guiding and helping others. First, so you understand the situation in which you find yourself, and then, so you find the courage to get out of it or, at least, so you know how to defend yourself while gathering the necessary strength to leave behind hurtful situations. I want to make sure that, if you put your mind to it, you can achieve it.

My situation seemed *almost* impossible, but I held on to the "almost" and, with God's help, I got it.

Today, I am a fulfilled woman in search of spiritual growth, something which would have been impossible to follow in an abusive relationship. I will tell you what I experienced, all the pain I had to endure, and what I learned along the way. I wrote this book with the need to break the silence that surrounds psychological and verbal abuse. By sharing stories, experiences, and resources, I want to empower women to acknowledge abuse, break free from their oppressors, and find the strength to rebuild their lives. I want every woman to know she is not alone, her voice matters, and she has the right and ability to live a life free from fear and control.

The phrase, "Break the Silence", is a call to action, empathy and solidarity. It is an invitation to all women to raise their voices, tell their stories, and join in the fight against abuse. Because every time a woman breaks the silence, a door to freedom opens for many others. Together, we can dismantle structures of oppression and build a world where every woman is valued, respected, and free.

Part I: My Testimony

I'll tell you stories of romance, which may seem like a mind-blowing drug. At first, we live an idyll where feelings and emotions reach feverishly high levels, and we believe that this will last forever. However, even in the most destructive relationships, the beginnings are often intense, full of emotions and expectations.

Over time, the woman begins to feel inadequate and uncomfortable, and her once-prosperous former life may be neglected or even abandoned.

My story begins when I met Mark at the age of twenty, on the beach. He was coming aboard an icebreaker ship from North America, on its way to Antarctica. My classmates and I were enjoying a break after a hectic college year, and although I didn't speak much English, my classmate struck up a conversation with him. Mark invited me to show him around the city, and I accepted.

The day we spent together was lovely. His kindness and patience with my English captivated me. Through letters, we kept in touch for more than a year, and when Mark returned to Chile, our relationship became more intimate. Despite noticing some irritations on his part, I ignored them, thinking it was normal.

One day, I received a call from a Mexican who informed me that Mark wanted to invite me to visit him in the United States, with all expenses paid. My mother insisted that I could only go if I was married and if he came to get me, which Mark accepted. Although I was excited, I also felt sad to leave everything I knew. However, the opportunity to move to the United States with Mark was tempting.

The first months in California were quiet. We lived at a friend of Mark's house before we moved into our own home. That's when I started noticing Mark's true character. His disproportionate reactions to my minor mistakes made me feel inadequate. I began to wonder why I couldn't do anything right for him. His behavior oscillated between calm and uncontrolled anger, and although I tried to understand him at first due to his painful past, the situation worsened.

Humiliations and verbal abuse became frequent, and Mark meticulously monitored me. At times, his fury was so intense that it endangered my life. You feel trapped in a dark corner, like a mouse curled up in its little shelter. Every time you try to move, you realize that your efforts are in vain, as if you are trapped in a labyrinth with no way out. Hopelessness takes over when you see that, no matter how hard you try, the situation remains the same, or even gets worse. The control you once thought you had has vanished, leaving you in a position where any attempt at change seems futile. You feel like you're caught in an invisible web that you can't break, and helplessness becomes a constant shadow that clouds your thoughts and feelings.

In the midst of this oppressive situation, loneliness becomes your most constant companion. Even though you're surrounded by people, you feel like no one really sees or understands you. It's as if you're isolated in a bubble of incomprehension, where attempts to communicate are absorbed by silence. This loneliness is not only an absence of company, but a profound disconnection with the outside world. Sometimes, you feel like you're watching life go by from a safe distance, without being able to participate or be a part of it. Loneliness becomes an emotional burden, a weight that you carry with you every moment of the day.

Every hurtful word and every act of contempt seems to reduce you to a shadow of what you used to be. Constant criticism and degrading comments have made you feel like you're no longer valuable, as if you've been stripped of your dignity and self-worth. Every day seems like a struggle to maintain a shred of your identity in the midst of a whirlwind of negativity and humiliation. The feeling of being demeaned becomes an open wound, one that never seems to fully heal. You feel that the space you are in limits you, and that any attempt to improve or get out of that situation is blocked by an invisible barrier of discouragement and contempt.

"Am I the crazy one?" was a recurring question that plunged me into inexplicable anguish. I had a big house, a vehicle, I was working and studying. Mark would take me for walks in the mountains and sometimes we would get together with his friends. However, he went from being calm to enraged, breaking things near me, as if to say, "The next one is you." Then, he would apologize and cry, saying that he had a lot of anger in his heart about the abuse he had witnessed in his home.

Over time, things got worse. Insults, disqualifications and humiliations became more frequent. Mark used even the slightest situations to control me. Once, I was late from work because of traffic and, in my desperation not to receive another humiliation, I decided to take a shortcut that led me to go in the wrong direction on a road, I thank God for the truck driver who honked his horn repeatedly, which made me realize the mistake and allowed me to correct the course. The humiliation I received that time was so strong, while trying to escape, I ended up on the edge of a ditch. When I got home, Mark yelled at me and said I was doing everything wrong. I felt scared and deeply lost.

I thought having a baby might calm him down, so I decided to get pregnant, and for a while, it seemed like it did. But by the fifth month my pregnancy became even more difficult when Mark demanded intimacy even though I was exhausted, leading to a complication that put our baby at risk.

He had to take me to the hospital, where the doctor prescribed medication to prevent contractions and absolute rest for the remainder of the pregnancy. Every day I went from the bed to the sofa to watch TV and he gave me breakfast, sometimes nutritious, sometimes not so much, depending on his good or bad mood. Then he went to work, leaving me there until he came back after 6pm and gave me some dinner that he brought since he didn't know how to cook or he opened a can or pre-cooked food from the freezer.

I called a colleague from school who brought me soup at noon that she took from the church where she belonged. I was very distressed and one day I told my mother, a great singer known in several countries, who decided to travel, leaving important commitments, from Chile to California to take care of me. I really didn't want to cause my mom any trouble, but I'm an only child and I had no choice but to let her come. It was a great relief to have my mother with me, so I felt less miserable. I tried to change my mood by thinking about my baby, enjoying my mother's presence and our pleasant talks, listening to beautiful music and reading interesting stories and books, but nevertheless when Mark was there it was very difficult since he not only made me feel bad but also my mom. She quickly understood my desperate situation.

She felt handcuffed because she thought she shouldn't get involved and that I was the one who had to make the determination to get out of there. She didn't want to influence my decision. She knew I had to decide for myself to leave the hell in which I lived, and she only perceived on the surface.

One day, Mark was sick with a cold, so he was more impatient than usual. My mother put something in the kitchen out of place, which provoked his fury, and he broke the door of one of the kitchen cabinets with a kick, screaming uncontrollably as many times before circling through his famous rosary of foul expletives. My mother was stunned, not knowing what to do. Witnessing this incident confirmed her suspicions. She was very distressed and worried.

I remained on bed rest until the eighth month of my pregnancy. One morning in March, my water broke, leaving me with no choice but to give birth to my baby. My friend who used to bring me soup from church picked me up to take me to the hospital and my mother accompanied me. There was a wait that seemed eternal. As soon as Mark could, he arrived. He was very impatient as the hours passed and I did not have my baby. I could see the expression on his face he always had when he was about to explode along with his usual gnashing of teeth.

My mother calmed me down and accompanied me as did the hospital staff.

Once my beautiful princess Victoria was home, everything seemed to get better for a while, he was sweeter and calmer, which gave me hope that things could change. This only lasted a few months. When my mother was preparing to return to Chile, I noticed her worry. She assured me she would always be there to support me and to take care of me a lot. She left heartbroken. I learned later, my friends told her not to leave me with that monster, but she couldn't do much when I didn't visualize my real situation and wouldn't dare to do something. I was left alone, hoping Mark would change. *Maybe now he was going to be okay, and we were going to be happy as a family.*

When I started working again, the pressure to meet Mark's expectations became even more difficult.

At fourth months old, Victoria began going to childcare during the day. It was very difficult for me to detach myself from my baby, but it was demanded of me by Mark and the system that exists in the United States where everyone has to work. Thankfully, the owner of the childcare was a guide and friend of mine who I knew from working as a nursing assistant. She was now taking care of several children, mainly from her family and my daughter. She and her husband are Victoria's Godparents.

After work, I couldn't delay even five minutes because Mark would get angry and breakout in a rage.

After Victoria's baptism, we had a dinner to celebrate, with her Godparents, family, and friends. I was sitting at the table and someone requested my presence. When I got up, I spilled my glass of wine by accident, which made Mark angry once again, this time in front of everyone leaving me very embarrassed and humiliated. He blurted out that I was useless and clumsy. He continued shouting and using profanity. The attendees excused themselves and left, but not before telling me more than once to call the police, which Mark apparently heard and began to calm down, apologizing to some guests who then decided to stay and dine with us. I think they stayed just so I was not left alone with him to escalate further. Again, he ruined everything.

Many times, I found myself sitting in a corner crying and feeling like the smallest creature in the universe, wondering what I was doing wrong and if all this was my fault. The confusion was overwhelming. His mood was unpredictable. The same things that made him laugh sometimes also infuriated him at other times. I had to be very careful *not* to do anything that would bother him. His attitude fluctuated from moment to moment. I didn't know what to think or do.

One particularly distressing event occurred when Mark became enraged over a minor accident with our car, leading to police intervention. My boss and colleagues noticed the situation, but out of fear, I couldn't report it.

In the midst of all this disaster, I found an angel named Ms. T. We were very close to one another at work. I thank her every day of my life. She saved my existence and is still my great friend. Ms. T was my direct boss in the bilingual area of the Livermore California School District. She decided to help me when she realized my terrible situation.

Many times, she told Mark I had to attend work meetings, while in reality, she took me to the mall or another nice place to have coffee and get me out of my hell for a while. Sometimes, other colleagues went with us. Those moments were wonderful. I felt free and esteemed by my friends; I forgot my pain for a couple of hours. However, I had to return to my reality and at the agreed time otherwise I would get into trouble.

On one occasion, Ms. T, my guardian angel in California, took the whole group of teachers to a weekend meeting and seminar, outside of

Livermore, to a city in Northern California. I personally related to many things shared in the seminar. I even talked to the psychologist who made the presentation, thinking he could advise me what to do to improve things in my marriage. But all he said to me was, "So? It will continue until you decide to stop putting up with it." I was really surprised and started to realize the urgency of my situation. I had to get out of that harmful relationship, but how?

It seemed almost impossible to me. I was a foreigner, married to an American, with a daughter, practically alone and I felt totally tied hand and foot.

More time passed. At this point, I had been in a relationship with Mark for six years. I endured a lot of psychological and verbal abuse. The only reason why it was not physical abuse was because Mark was respectful (fearful) of authority and knew that he could more easily go to jail if he hit me. Wounds and bruises are physical evidence. The verbal and psycho-logical abuse at that time had no validity so it was impossible for me to prove he really abused me.

I was on the verge of collapse, but I kept hoping that something magical would happen. In the sixth year, something happened that finally made me decide to find a way to get out of there and return to Chile with my mother and my paternal family. I took an opportunity to join a prestigious beauty line and started a small business selling creams and makeup. One afternoon I was arranging some boxes filled with beauty products and doing accounts in the guest room where I had a small desk and kept everything related to the business. As Mark laid on the bed waiting for me to finish, Victoria began to jump on it when suddenly she accidentally hit Mark's nose hard. He stood up indignant, screamed furiously, and yelled profanity. He lifted the chair from the desk and broke it by hitting it very close to where my boxes were. I was terrified and Victoria noticed it immediately and was fearful. I said in a low voice, "Oh, he is going to break my creams!" My daughter heard me and screamed at her father to leave her mother alone. I hugged her immediately and for a moment I expected the worst for the two of us, but by some miracle of God, Mark left the room where we remained trembling, especially me. It was at that moment I said to myself, "Enough! Enough of all this!" I could put up with many things, but it was not up to my daughter to defend me, especially from such an early age, I asked myself, "Now she is three years old, what is going to happen at seven or fourteen years old?" Every option that came to mind was horrific. Violence, death, jail, or I end up taking my life like Mark's mother did. It was at this very moment, I received the courage to say, "I have to go now!"

My goal was to investigate, think, and analyze how I could get out without costing my daughter and me our lives. I spoke with Ms. T. She immediately gave me all her support. We met at her house with another colleague and called a lawyer, since the first consultation was free. We presented my case, and she advised me of the possibilities I had. Fortunately, the year before this decision we made had plans to travel as a family out of the country, so we got a passport for my daughter. That specific trip did not take place, but now the passport would allow me to travel with Victoria.

With the help of Ms. T and other friends, I began preparing for our departure. Ms. T planned for us to go to San Francisco, California to register Victoria at the Chilean Consulate, which was fantastic since it simplified her legal stay in Chile. It felt like everything was aligned and flowing. We had a real chance to get away.

The lawyer advised me to leave him a letter telling him I was going to see my mother and rest, since I was very nostalgic and tired, I would be gone awhile, and I did not tell him ahead of time because I knew he would refuse to let me go. I included an address and telephone number, like the lawyers said, in case he wanted to locate me.

With those pieces in place, I began to call travel agencies in my free time at work for tickets. I finally found a flight in a reasonable timeframe to finalize everything without him knowing. It was exciting and at the same time terrifying. I informed Ms. T and she bought the tickets for me, but not before making sure *it* was what I really wanted to do. She told me to wait to pay her back for the cost of the tickets until my last day here so Mark would not notice the bank transaction. That was a great idea, and I was thankful! My next dilemma was getting our things out of the house without arousing Mark's suspicion.

I spoke with a student I taught Spanish to and became friends with about my situation. She wanted to help me and said I could use her suitcases to pack me and Victoria's belongings. She worked from home on her computer, so she was available any time to take us to the airport. I was extremely grateful because the airport was an hour's drive away in San Francisco and none of my friends or colleagues were available. I was relieved that I did not have to use various modes of public transportation carrying luggage with my child.

The days before the trip seemed eternal, my nerves were destroyed, I didn't have much appetite, and it was difficult for me to sleep imagining Mark could realize my intentions and the terrible consequences if he found out.

You may be wondering: *Why escape?* I believe it was the only possible solution for me and my daughter since I was terrified of Mark. I felt my only options were to escape or suffer unthinkable and terrifying consequences. I endured his innumerable outbursts, but when they started to more frequently involve Victoria, I knew I had to take action. On one occasion when I was not there but my mother was, Mark hit Victoria on her very small buttocks and left the area red. I was afraid to report it and I prayed to heaven it would not happen again. Mark justified his action by reminding me I should have been home earlier from my work meeting.

Finally, the long-awaited day arrived, and I took Victoria to Kindergarten earlier than usual. When I returned Mark was still at home and had little desire to go to work. I was in shock. I tried to persuade him to leave and began to do things around the house just like it was a normal day. I even prepared to go to work, even though Ms. T knew I had already formally resigned. It was strange. It seemed like he sensed something was going to happen.

Finally, he went to work. I had to take a couple of suitcases out of the garage to put the last things most dear to Victoria in, such as toys, movies, and books. I started packing at full speed, I called my friend to take me to the bank, so I could return the money to Ms. T. Next, I returned to Victoria's Kindergarten, and told the school there was an urgent family problem. We unexpectedly had to leave town, and our flight was departing at one o'clock.

The day before when I was with Ms. T at work, we said our goodbyes, and promised to see each other one day in better circumstances. We hugged each other in an eternal embrace full of tenderness and on my side gratitude. She gave me two books that have been a light on my path. One is authored by Dr. Susan Forward and it helped me to discover the reality of my situation. It has also inspired and guided me to tell my story and write this book to be able to help many other women who are going through the same or similar things to what I went through. The day I finally left, I felt a mixture of terror and relief. As I walked away from the house I had shared with Mark, I couldn't help but cry. Although I was scared, I also felt a freedom that I hadn't experienced in a long time.

We arrived at the airport just in time to make our flight. I thanked my friend from the bottom of my heart. Victoria and I got on the plane expectant and very nervous until it finally took off. I felt a relief that I can't describe, it was like a huge weight lifted off my shoulders. I felt free and filled with a lot of hope that everything was going to be much better. I must emphasize that my daughter, who already communicated well and who knew who her father was, at no time questioned why we were leaving. She never asked, "Where is my daddy?" or said, "I want to go home." This revealed to me, Victoria had a level of understanding and empathy greater than her age of three and a half years old. It was as if she sensed how bad her mother felt about this man.

It took me about ten years to recover from everything that happened. Psychological and verbal abuse are so cruel and very difficult to overcome, although misogynists are now a better-known topic than back then, during the nineties.

> **Misogynist:** (n.) a person who hates or discriminates against women: a misogynistic person[1]

When I arrived in Chile at the age of thirty and dejected, there were not many psychologists to help me. When I went to consult with one, he complimented me on my bravery to escape, and did not think I needed further help. He did not consider for a moment the lingering consequences of the abuse. Then I went to talk to a priest, as my mother advised, and he told me that perhaps it had been me who caused the situation, which left me even worse, feeling very guilty of, according to him, breaking up a family.

Meanwhile, Mark continued to call me, sometimes furious and at other times loving, begging me, and even crying. This made me feel even more guilty, until I realized that it was part of the psychological management, so I told him I still did not want to return. The truth is, I did not plan to ever return, but if I managed to keep him believing I would eventually come back, I figured he would not come to force me or take away my daughter, which was what worried me the most.

At night, while my daughter slept, I dedicated myself to reading Dr. Susan Forward's book. I could not understand how some of the people she referenced endured abuse for as many as thirty years. I cried inconsolably for myself and for all those women who did not manage to get out and lived a life of hell, so I vowed to write this book to help those who are living it now and to prevent others from living it.

Once in Chile, I began to rebuild my life. At first, everything seemed overwhelming. I was alone in a country where a single mother was not well regarded at the time. However, over time, I began to find my way. I received help from local organizations which support women in abusive situations. I attended alternative therapies and began to talk openly about what I had experienced. This process was painful, but also profoundly liberating. Through therapy, I began to understand that what I had experienced was not my fault. The abuse was not a consequence of my actions, but of Mark's insecurities and need for control. This allowed me to begin to heal and regain my self-esteem.

My faith also played a pivotal role in my recovery. I clung to the idea that God had a purpose for me, and that my experience could be used to help other women. Little by little, I began to see my life with a new perspective. What I had experienced did not define me. Ultimately, what mattered was how I decided to move forward.

I spent many years living in fear that Mark would kidnap my daughter or take legal action to take her from me. I took every necessary safeguard, including at the school she attended, and every place we spent time. I did everything in my power to protect Victoria. I assure you, it was not a pleasant lifestyle, but it was some of the price I paid for escaping like I did. My mother's friends helped ensure at the national level that Victoria could not leave the country (Arraigo Nacional), which prevented me from leaving too for a while, but I didn't care.

After time passed, I was able to go and spend a few years in Miami, renew my residency, and return to Chile without any problem. Like any process, it took a while, but it all came together through patience and perseverance.

As I regained my life, I also began to reconnect with my family and friends. Their unconditional support was vital to my healing process. I realized that even though I had been isolated for so long, I was never really alone. There were always people willing to help me, but I had to take the first step and ask for help.

One of the most difficult moments was facing the emotional aftermath of abuse. Often, I felt invaded by painful memories and a feeling that I would never be good enough. However, I learned to recognize these thoughts as part of the healing process. I accepted that I had the right to feel sad, angry, and frustrated, but I also had the right to be happy and to build a life full of love and respect.

I remade my life the year after I returned to Chile with an ex-boyfriend from the university who supported, cared for, and helped me for years and with whom I had a beautiful girl, my second princess, now turned into a young lady. This relationship lasted for 16 years. I realized I had not had a chance to develop as a person, before I entered into this new relationship, after my ordeal with Mark. I was not healthy, and I had not recovered as a person. What I did was put myself on autopilot and pretend to have a happy life. This was not fair to our family, and we mistreated our relationship. I gave my new partner all my will and decision making. For a long time, I ignored my spiritual and emotional growth. I stayed in this relationship for a long time to give my daughters a home, but it hurt us, and we are still recovering.

My great advice when starting a new relationship, after managing to get out of the clutches of a misogynist, it is to fully heal in every aspect, and allow a considerable amount of time to pass. Often, even one or two years, are not enough time to undo all the trauma and heal, especially if a person is not treated by a psychologist or therapist. Later, in this book, I give keys on how to identify this type of relationship and provide guidance to end the relationship or put boundaries in place, to mend the relationship, if a person does not want to leave.

Despite all I shared in my story and the experiences I had, my two daughters are the best thing in my life, along with my mother and grandchildren. They are my pillars and my great loves. I am very proud of them. I love them dearly and I will never regret having conceived them. I think they are a divine gift.

Now after years of my separation, I have learned to be happy alone. I have regained my independence, make my own decisions, and am dedicated to my family, to my alternative therapies, and to writing.

My greatest desire, with all my heart, is that my testimony and that of other women which I share in this book, in addition to the research I have included to provide understanding, strategies, and resources, give readers the light and courage needed to get out of life's storms and even violent relationships. I genuinely offer essential guidance and support to help free victims and their children from the yoke of those who suffer from misogyny.

My testimony is proof that the courage needed to get out of an abusive relationship is inside of us and the importance of seeking help and support.

Today, I look back and see how far I've come. What was once a dark and painful period in my life is now a source of strength and wisdom. My experience has taught me to value myself and never accept less than I deserve. I know that my story can help other women see that there is a way out, that they are not alone, and that they have the strength to break free.

Part II: Understanding the Root of Abuse

*Organizations mentioned in this section to support claims are identified in the Recommended Books & Websites for Additional Support, beginning on page 127.

Below, I lay out what I have learned and how it has clarified my understanding of the cases of abuse I have experienced and observed in many women who have not been fortunate enough to recognize and escape in time from a life of suffering and pain.

As I mentioned earlier, I drew from a book by Dr. Susan Forward titled, *Men Who Hate Women and the Women Who Love Them: When Loving Hurts and You Don't Know Why.*[1] It explains that an abuser usually comes from a past where he or she has been repeatedly abused by his or her parents or caregivers. This past of abuse contributes to very low self-esteem, leaving them with a deep inner pain bringing constant torment. To alleviate this pain, the abuser seeks a victim onto whom to project their own suffering, aiming to make the victim feel worse than themself in order to experience a brief, palliative drug-like relief from pain.

The Root of Low Self-Esteem in Abusers

The true root of low self-esteem in abusers can be traced to the experiences lived with their mothers. Four types of mothers are identified below that can contribute to the development of an abuser:

- **The Abused Mother**: This mother has been the victim of various types of abuse—verbal, psychological, physical, sexual, and/or monetary. Their inability or unwill-ingness to defend themselves or change their abusive situation, due to fear or intimidation, results in their child(ren) internalizing severe and cruel misogyny. This type of mother perpetuates a cycle of abuse and submission that deeply affects her child(ren)'s psychology.
- **The Indifferent or Absent Mother**: Even if this mother is physically present, their

lack of emotional or psychological involve-ment can be harmful. Their disinterest in their child(ren)'s conflicts and problems, or immersion in their own pain, contributes to the formation of a misogynistic attitude in their child(ren), who may feel that his or her emotional needs are not important.

- **The Overprotective Mother**: This type of mother prevents the development of independence by suffocating their child-(ren) with excessive protection. This lack of autonomy can lead the child to feel incapable and useless, cultivating frus-tration and resentment that can manifest itself in abusive behaviors towards others.
- **The Authoritarian and Abusive Mother**: This mother exercises control In an authoritarian and abusive manner, often using verbal and psychological abuse. Harsh discipline and contemptuous treat-ment can result in a distorted view of relationships and respect for others, fostering misogynistic and abusive atti-tudes in their child(ren).

Implications of the Past on the Abuser's Behavior

These different types of parenting contribute to the formation of an individual who, feeling small and hurt, seeks to externalize their pain.

Abusers, therefore, often come from contexts of personal abuse and look to their relationships for a way to replicate and project their own suffering. This results in a cycle of abuse where the victim becomes the receptacle of the abuser's unresolved distress.

Understanding these mechanisms is crucial to addressing the problem of abuse from a deeper and more effective perspective. Recognizing the influence of the family environment and parenting patterns can provide a foundation for intervention and prevention strategies that address both the aftermath of abuse and its roots.

Definition of Misogynist

The term "misogynist" refers to a person, usually a man (although it can also be applied to women, although it is less common), who develops a deep duality in their relationship with the female sex. This duality manifests as a "Love-Hate" relationship towards the mother figure who gave birth to him.

According to Dr. Susan Forward, the most accurate definition of misogynist is "hatred of women." The Greek word for "woman hater": *misogynist*, from *miso*, meaning "to hate," and *gyne*, meaning "woman."[2]

Often, the term is misinterpreted as a simple characteristic of a liar or manipulator, but in reality, it is something much deeper and more destructive. Dr. Forward, in her research, found that misogynists fall into a similar category to serial killers and psychopaths, given the intensity and cruelty of their behavior.

This behavior becomes even more dramatic when a misogynistic man maintains a stable relationship. In this context, women can undergo a radical transformation due to abuse. A woman who was previously successful, active, and self-confident may become someone without willpower, without the ability to make decisions, and who may even suffer physical changes such as weight gain and self-neglect, all for fear of a violent reaction from her partner.

Violence can be physical, or manifest itself through material damage, psychological or verbal threats, varying according to the social and economic context.

Often, the woman in this situation does not realize her condition until she reaches a critical point of despair and depression, feeling trapped with no way out.

The Reality of Psychological and Verbal Abuse

Psychological and verbal abuse are insidious forms of violence that often go unnoticed. Unlike physical abuse, which leaves visible marks, psychological abuse slowly erodes the victim's self-esteem and well-being. It is a form of control that is exercised through hurtful words, emotional manipulations and coercive behaviors.[3]

Women who suffer this type of abuse usually feel trapped, as if there is no escape. The abuser often uses tactics such as gaslighting (making the victim doubt their own perception of reality), social isolation (alienating them from friends and family), and constant degradation (making them feel worthless without them). These patterns of behavior are designed to destroy the victim's autonomy, leaving them dependent and devoid of the confidence necessary to seek help.

The impact of psychological and verbal abuse is profound. Victims may experience depression, anxiety, sleep disturbances, and a general loss of the ability to enjoy life. Constant fear and the feeling that everything they do is wrong can paralyze them, preventing them from making the necessary decisions to change their situation.

It is crucial to understand that psychological and verbal abuse is no less serious than physical abuse. Although it does not leave visible scars, its effects are long-lasting and can be devastating. Victims need support, understanding, and often professional help to break the cycle of abuse and rebuild their lives.[4]

How to Identify Psychological and Verbal Abuse

The first step to freedom from abuse is to acknowledge it. However, due to the insidious nature of psychological and verbal abuse, many women don't realize they are being mistreated until the damage is done. Here are some signs that you might be in an abusive relationship:

- **Constant criticism**: Your partner criticizes you for everything from how you dress to how you talk. Nothing you do seems to be good enough for him.
- **Emotional manipulation**: Your partner uses your emotions against you. He makes you feel guilty about things that aren't your fault or punishes you emotionally when you don't do what he wants.

- **Isolation**: Your partner takes you away from your friends and family, making you depend solely on him for emotional support.
- **Gaslighting**: Your partner distorts reality to make you doubt your own perceptions and judgments. It makes you believe that you are crazy or that you are irrational.
- **Excessive control**: Your partner controls every aspect of your life, from your finances to who you can talk to. You feel like you can't make decisions for yourself.

If you recognize any of these behaviors in your relationship, it's important to seek help. You're not alone, and there are resources available to help you get out of an abusive relationship.

The Cycle of Abuse

The cycle of abuse is a dynamic that repeats itself in relationships and is a process that can be difficult to break due to its cyclical and deceptive nature. This cycle has been extensively documented in psychological literature and is generally composed of three main phases:

- **Tension and Disagreement**: During this phase, tensions build up within the relationship. These conflicts may start as minor disagreements, but the abuser uses emotional manipulation tactics and constant criticism to escalate the tension. Studying domestic violence, identified that the victim at this stage usually experiences great anxiety and fear, seeking to avoid any behavior that could trigger a violent reaction from the abuser. This constant fear contributes to the creation of a toxic psychological environment.

- **Incident of Abuse**: This phase is the climax of the cycle, where the abuse occurs. It can manifest itself in a variety of ways, including physical, verbal, emotional, or psychological abuse. According to statistics from the National Coalition Against Domestic Violence (NCADV), in the United States, 85% of reported cases of domestic violence include a significant component of psychological abuse. During this incident, the abuser exerts their control through abuse, which can leave the victim in a state of extreme desperation and vulnerability.

- **Reconciliation and Honeymoon**: After the incident, the abuser usually tries to repair the relationship through a reconciliation phase, showing regret and promising to change. This phase is highly deceptive, as the abuser may behave in a loving and caring manner, leading the victim to believe that the abusive behavior will not occur again. However, this phase is a temporary component of the abuse cycle and the relationship soon returns to the tension phase, restarting the cycle.

Psychological Impact on the Victim

Psychological abuse is defined as a pattern of behavior that seeks to control, manipulate, and dominate a person by exploiting their emotions and fears. Unlike physical abuse, which manifests itself through visible injuries, psychological abuse manifests itself through tactics of belittlement, humiliation, and isolation.

On the other hand, verbal abuse involves the use of words and expressions to degrade and denigrate the victim. It can include name-calling, threats, and derogatory comments that undermine the person's self-esteem and confidence.

Psychological and Emotional Impacts of Abuse

Psychological and verbal abuse can have profound and lasting effects on victims' mental health. Studies have shown that victims of psychological abuse experience an increase in the prevalence of disorders such as anxiety, depression, and post-traumatic stress disorder (PTSD).

A study conducted by the National Institute of Mental Health in 2019 showed that women who had experienced psychological abuse were nearly twice as likely to experience severe depression compared to those who had not. In addition, psychological abuse is associated with an increased risk of suicide attempts, addiction problems, and eating disorders.

The psychological impact of abuse can be devastating and far-reaching. Victims can experience a number of emotional and psychological effects, including:

- **Low Self-Esteem**: Constant abuse undermines the victim's self-esteem, making them feel belittled and incapable. The victim may begin to doubt their own worth and abilities.
- **Anxiety and Depression**: Constant tension and abuse can lead the victim to develop severe anxiety and depression. Feelings of hopelessness and an inability to escape the situation can intensify these symptoms.
- **Distrust and Isolation**: Victims of abuse may develop a deep distrust of others and withdraw from friends and family. Social isolation is a tactic that the abuser uses to maintain control and make it difficult for the victim to receive support from others, even people they were previously close to.
- **Physical Health Problems**: The prolonged stress of abuse can have physical

consequences, such as sleep disturbances, gastrointestinal problems, and
chronic pain. The victim's physical health
can deteriorate due to constant emotional
stress and abuse.

Breaking the Cycle

Breaking the cycle of abuse is a challenging but
an essential process for recovery and well-
being. Here are some tips:

- **Acknowledge the Abuse**: The first step
  is to acknowledge that you are in an
  abusive relationship. Accepting the
  reality of abuse is crucial to begin
  seeking help and support. Studies have
  shown that awareness of abuse is the
  critical first step in breaking the cycle.
  According to the American Psychological
  Association, 70% of victims who acknowledge abuse seek help.
- **Seek Professional Support**: It is essential
  to seek the help of trained professionals,
  such as psychologists, therapists, and
  counselors specialized in abuse. They can

provide coping strategies, emotional support, and help with the recovery process. Cognitive Behavioral Therapy (CBT) has been shown to be effective in helping victims regain their self-esteem and break the cycle of abuse.[5]

- **Set Boundaries**: It is important to set clear boundaries with the abuser and communicate firmly what will not be tolerated. Self-affirmation and setting clear boundaries can help the victim regain control of their life.

- **Seek a Support Network**: Having the support of friends, family, and specialty groups can provide crucial assistance during the process of leaving an abusive relationship. A support network can offer emotional and practical security.

- **Plan a Safe Exit**: In cases of physical or serious abuse, it is essential to plan a safe exit. This may include preparing an emergency plan, finding a safe place to stay, and seeking legal assistance if necessary. Preparation, when possible, with the support of specialized professionals and organizations, is essential for victims who are in high-risk situations.

Survival Strategies and Support

It is crucial that victims of psychological and verbal abuse seek support and use effective strategies to overcome trauma. Interventions include psychological therapy, social support, and, in some cases, legal measures to protect the victim from future abuse.[6]

Characteristics and Comparison of Psychological and Verbal Abuse

Psychological Abuse manifests through a variety of tactics that seek to control, manipulate, and degrade the victim:

- **Disqualification**: Minimization or ridicule of the victim's opinions and feelings, making them feel inferior and insignificant.
- **Control**: The abuser uses coercive tactics to control the victim's thoughts, behaviors, and decisions.

- **Isolation**: Limiting or severing the victim's ties with their support network, leaving them emotionally dependent on the abuser.
- **Gaslighting**: Psychological manipulation that causes the victim to doubt their own perception and judgment, undermining their self-confidence.

Verbal Abuse, on the other hand, includes the use of derogatory and offensive language to degrade and humiliate the victim. This type of abuse can include:

- **Insults and Threats**: Use of hurtful words and threats to intimidate and control the victim.
- **Contempt**: Derogatory comments designed to undermine the victim's self-esteem and make them feel worthless.

Interventions and Public Policies

To effectively address the problem of psychological and verbal abuse, interventions need to be implemented at the individual, community, and government levels. Here are some research-based strategies and best practices:

- **Prevention Programs**: Prevention is key to reducing the incidence of psychological and verbal abuse. Educational programs in schools and communities that teach about healthy relationships and acknowledgment of abuse can be effective in adolescents significantly reducing tolerant attitudes toward violence in relationships.
- **Training of Health Professionals**: Health professionals play a crucial role in identifying and supporting victims of abuse. Training doctors, nurses, and therapists to spot signs of psychological and verbal abuse can improve rates of early intervention and victim support.
- **Protection Policies and Legislation**: It is essential that laws and public policies support victims of psychological and verbal abuse. This includes implementing laws that recognize psychological abuse as a form of domestic violence and that provide adequate protections. In many countries,

efforts are underway to update laws to include psychological and emotional abuse in the legal definition of domestic violence. An example of this is legislation in the United Kingdom, where the Domestic Abuse Act 2021 includes "coercive and controlling behaviour" as a punishable offence.[7]

- **Victim Support Services**: Providing access to safe shelters, helplines, and specialized counseling is essential to helping victims escape abusive situations. Organizations like the National Domestic Violence Hotline in the U.S. offer 24-hour resources and support for people experiencing abuse.

International Context

To give a more global context to the problem of psychological and verbal abuse, here are some international statistics:

- According to a World Health Organization (WHO) study, 48% of women who have been physically abused have also suffered psychological abuse.

- According to the United Nations (UN), 23% of women dating globally have experienced some form of psychological or verbal abuse.
- In Latin America, a report by the Economic Commission for Latin America and the Caribbean (ECLAC) reveals that between 40% and 60% of women have been victims of psychological abuse at some point in their lives.
- In Europe, the European Union Agency for Fundamental Rights estimates approximately 43% of women have experienced some form of psychological abuse by their intimate partner.

Conclusion

Psychological and verbal abuse is an insidious form of violence that causes deep and lasting damage to victims. It is vital that society as a whole recognizes the seriousness of this type of abuse and that effective measures are taken to prevent, identify, and treat it. Victims need not only emotional and psychological support, but also a legal and social system that protects them and helps them rebuild their lives.

Risk Factors and Vulnerability

It is important to understand that certain risk factors can make some people more vulnerable to psychological and verbal abuse. These factors do not justify abuse, but they help to understand why some people may be more susceptible to becoming victims or perpetrators of this type of violence.

- **History of Abuse**: People who have been victims of abuse during childhood or who have grown up in a violent environment are at a higher risk of experiencing or perpetuating abuse in their adult relationships. A study by the American Psychological Association (APA) found that 30% of adults who were abused in their childhood repeat these patterns in their intimate relationships.

- **Economic Dependence**: Victims who are financially dependent on their abuser have more difficulty leaving the relationship. Economic dependence can cause a victim to tolerate abuse for fear of not being able to support themselves, which perpetuates the cycle of abuse.
- **Low Self-Esteem and Self-Efficacy**: Low self-esteem and lack of confidence in one's ability to make changes can increase vulnerability to abuse. Victims who feel they don't deserve better treatment or don't have the ability to get out of the abusive relationship are less likely to seek help.
- **Sociocultural Factors**: In many cultures, gender norms and expectations may contribute to the tolerance of abuse. Societies that promote women's submission and male domination tend to have higher rates of domestic abuse. A report by the World Health Organization (WHO) stresses that attitudes that tolerate gender-based violence are associated with higher levels of psychological and verbal abuse.

- **Resistance to Change:** The pressure to fulfill traditional family roles can make women reluctant to challenge the status quo. Even when they acknowledge the abuse, they may feel that by doing so they are violating their responsibilities as wives and mothers. This resistance to change may be rooted in fear of social disapproval, loss of identity, and fear of retaliation from the abuser.

Psychological and Therapeutic Interventions

Psychological interventions are essential for the recovery of victims of psychological and verbal abuse. These interventions should be tailored to each victim's individual needs and may include a variety of therapeutic approaches:

- **Cognitive Behavioral Therapy (CBT):** CBT is a form of therapy that has been shown to be effective in treating trauma associated with abuse. It helps victims identify and challenge negative thought patterns that have been internalized through abuse and found to be highly effective in reducing symptoms of PTSD, anxiety, and depression in victims of abuse.

- **Group Therapy**: Participating in support groups with other victims of abuse can be therapeutic and empowering. Support groups provide a safe space where victims can share their experiences, receive validation, and learn from each other's coping strategies. In addition, these groups can reduce social isolation, one of the most damaging effects of psychological abuse.

- **Eye Movement Desensitization and Reprocessing (EMDR) Therapy**: EMDR is an evidence-based therapy used to treat trauma. It is especially helpful for victims of psychological abuse who have developed PTSD. EMDR helps process and desensitize traumatic memories, allowing victims to move forward in their recovery.[8]

- **Psychosocial Interventions**: Combining psychological support with social resources, such as legal help and access to community services, can be very effective. These integrated interventions address not only emotional trauma, but also the practical barriers that prevent victims from escaping abuse.

Legal and Protection Resources

Access to legal and protective remedies is vital for victims seeking to escape an abusive relationship. These resources may include:

- **Protective Orders**: Legal tools that can restrict the abuser from approaching the victim. These orders are essential for victims who are in immediate danger or who fear for their safety.
- **Legal Assistance**: Accessing free or low-cost legal assistance to victims is crucial, especially for those facing economic barriers. Domestic violence attorneys can help victims navigate the legal system, including obtaining orders of protection, child custody, and divorce.

The Importance of Ongoing Research

Finally, it is essential to continue researching psychological and verbal abuse to better understand its dynamics and develop more effective interventions. Research should focus on:

- **New Forms of Abuse**: With the advancement of technology, new forms of psychological abuse have emerged, such as cyberbullying and abuse through social networks. It is crucial that researchers explore these dynamics to develop prevention and support strategies.
- **Effectiveness of Interventions**: Continuing to evaluate the effectiveness of current interventions is critical to ensuring that victims receive the best possible support. This includes longitudinal studies that follow victims over time to measure the outcomes of different types of intervention.
- **Social and Economic Impact**: Understanding the social and economic impact of psychological and verbal abuse can help policymakers allocate resources more effectively. Research that quantifies the costs associated with healthcare, lost productivity, and social services can be

useful in advocating for more funding and support programs.

Impact on Children and Adolescents

Children and adolescents who grow up in homes where there is psychological and verbal abuse, either as witnesses or as direct victims, can suffer serious and long-term consequences on their emotional, social, and psychological development.

- **Emotional Development**: Children who witness psychological abuse between their parents or who are direct victims of it can develop emotional problems such as anxiety, depression, and low self-esteem. These children often internalize violence, coming to believe that it is a normal part of relationships, which can perpetuate a cycle of violence in their own adult lives.
- **Academic Performance**: The tense environment and constant stress can negatively affect children's academic performance. It is common for children exposed to abuse to have difficulty concentrating, behavioral

problems in school, and an increased risk of dropping out of school.

- **Interpersonal relationships**: Teens who have grown up in an abusive environment may have difficulty forming healthy relationships. They may replicate patterns of abuse in their own romantic relationships, or develop a deep distrust of others, which prevents them from making genuine emotional connections.
- **Long-Term Mental Health**: Studies have shown that children and adolescents who have been exposed to psychological abuse have a higher risk of developing mental disorders throughout their lives, including personality disorders, emotional regulation problems, and self-injurious behaviors.
- **The "Broken Home" Myth:** A common myth is that it's better for children to grow up in a home with both parents, even if one parent is abusive. This belief can lead victims to remain in dangerous relation-ships under the assumption that they are doing the right thing for their children. However, research has shown that children

who grow up in abusive environments can suffer serious emotional and psychological consequences, and that separation from a toxic environment can, in fact, be beneficial for them.

Cultural and Systemic Barriers to Reporting Abuse

Despite the severity of psychological and verbal abuse, many victims face significant barriers to reporting it and seeking help. These barriers can be cultural, social, or systemic in nature.

- **Cultural Norms**: In many cultures, there is a stigma associated with reporting abuse, especially when it occurs within the family. Cultural norms that value discretion, family honor, or that promote submission in relationships can deter victims from talking openly about their situation. A report by the United Nations Population Fund (UNFPA) highlights how cultural beliefs can perpetuate gender-based violence and make intervention more difficult.

- **Distrust of Authorities**: Many victims of abuse do not trust authorities, such as the police or the judicial system, to protect or provide support. This distrust may be based on previous experiences of in-effectiveness, discrimination, or fear of retaliation, which leaves victims feeling powerless and isolated.
- **Lack of Resources**: In some communities, especially in rural or impoverished areas, there may be a lack of resources and services accessible to victims of abuse. The lack of shelters, free legal services, and psychological support can leave victims feeling like they have nowhere else to turn.
- **Legal Barriers**: In many countries, laws against psychological and verbal abuse are limited or non-existent. Even where they exist, victims may face legal barriers, such as difficulty proving abuse in the absence of physical evidence, which can discourage reporting.
- **Fear of Losing Custody:** Some victims fear that if they leave their partner, they

could lose custody of their children. This fear may be exacerbated by threats from the abuser, who may claim they will fight for custody or use other legal tactics to separate the victim from their children. This type of manipulation is a powerful form of control that can keep the victim trapped in the relationship.

- **Financial Wellness Concern:** Economic stability is a major concern for many victims, especially if the abuser is the family's primary financial provider. The idea of maintaining the family unit may be motivated by the fear of not being able to financially support the children on their own, which reinforces the victim's economic and emotional dependence on the abuser.

The Role of Public Policies

Public policies are fundamental for the prevention of psychological and verbal abuse and the protection of victims. Governments can play a crucial role by implementing laws and support programs, as well as promoting cultural changes.

- **Comprehensive Legislation**: It is essential that laws recognize and punish psychological and verbal abuse as a form of domestic violence. This includes creating legal mechanisms that allow victims to obtain protection orders, access to support services, and justice for the harm they suffer. Countries such as Spain and Australia have made progress in enacting laws that explicitly recognize psychological abuse in their penal codes.

- **Support Programs**: Governments can fund programs that provide comprehensive support to victims, including shelters, free legal advice, and access to psychological care. It is also important that these programs are accessible to all victims, regardless of their economic situation or geographic location.

- **Education & Raising Awareness**: Nationwide awareness campaigns can change societal attitudes towards psychological and verbal abuse, educating the public about its seriousness and encouraging victims to seek help. In addition, including violence education in the school curriculum can prevent future cases of abuse by teaching young people about mutual respect and healthy relationships.

- **Multisectoral Collaboration**: Combating psychological and verbal abuse requires the collaboration of multiple sectors, including health, justice, education, and social services. Governments can facilitate this collaboration by creating cross-sectoral frameworks that ensure victims receive coherent and coordinated support.
- **Education in Schools and Communities:** Prevention education is critical to breaking the cycle of abuse in future generations. Educational programs in schools, universities, and communities can teach about healthy relationships, consent, and the dangers of machismo and restrictive gender norms. These initiatives can also empower young people to identify and reject abusive behaviors from an early age.

Importance of International Support

Psychological and verbal abuse is not a problem isolated to a single country or culture; It is a global phenomenon that requires an international response. Bodies such as the United Nations and the World Health Organization have recognized the importance of addressing this type of abuse as a violation of human rights.

- **International Conventions**: International treaties such as the Convention on the Elimination of All Forms of Discrimination against Women (CEDAW) urge countries to take action against gender-based violence, including psychological and verbal abuse. These conventions provide a framework for countries to implement policies and laws that protect victims.[9]

- **International Assistance and Cooperation**: Countries can benefit from international cooperation to share best practices, resources, and technical support in the fight against abuse. Financial and technical assistance can be crucial in helping countries with fewer resources implement effective prevention and support programs.

- **Global Monitoring and Evaluation**: It is essential that the international community monitors and assesses progress in the fight against psychological and verbal abuse globally. This includes collecting data, evaluating the effectiveness of policies, and identifying areas where more action is needed.

Psychological and Verbal Abuse Prevention Strategies

Preventing psychological and verbal abuse requires a proactive approach that involves individuals, communities, and governments. Prevention strategies are critical to creating an environment where mutual respect is promoted and violence in all its forms is eradicated.

- **Education in Schools**: Introducing emotional and healthy relationship education programs in schools can be a powerful tool to prevent abuse from an early age. These programs can teach children and teens about the importance of respectful communication, conflict management, and recognizing signs of abuse in relationships.

- **Training for Professionals**: It is crucial that professionals who work in contact with potential victims of abuse, such as teachers, social workers, doctors, and police officers, receive training on how to identify and address psychological and verbal abuse. Training should include how to provide appropriate support and refer victims to appropriate services.

- **Public Awareness Campaigns**: Large-scale awareness campaigns can help change social attitudes and denormalize psychological and verbal abuse. These campaigns can use traditional and digital media to educate the public about what constitutes abuse, how it affects victims, and where to seek help.

- **Promoting Gender Equality**: Gender inequality is one of the roots of abuse in relationships. Promoting gender equality through public policies, community programs, and cultural changes is essential to reducing psychological and verbal abuse. This includes fighting against gender stereotypes that perpetuate control and domination in relationships.

- **Strengthening Community Support Networks**: Creating support networks in communities can be an effective strategy to prevent abuse. These networks may include victim support groups, hotlines, and community centers where people can go for counseling and guidance.
- **Empowerment of Potential Victims**: Empowering people at risk of being victims of abuse, especially women and youth, is crucial for prevention. Programs that focus on developing assertiveness, economic independence, and rights awareness skills can help reduce vulnerability to abuse.

Research and Data Collection

A strong database and evidence is crucial to addressing psychological and verbal abuse effectively. Research in this field not only helps to better understand the problem, but also provides the information needed to design policies and intervention programs.

- **National Data Collection**: It is essential for countries to further implement national data collection systems that capture the prevalence of psychological and verbal abuse. This data should be disaggregated by gender, age, and other relevant factors to identify high-risk patterns and groups.
- **Academic Research**: Universities and research centers can play a crucial role in the study of psychological and verbal abuse. Research can explore areas such as risk factors, long-term consequences, and the effectiveness of different interventions.
- **Program Evaluation**: It is important that prevention and intervention programs and policies are evaluated on a regular basis to ensure their effectiveness. This includes assessing whether programs are reaching target populations and whether they are having the desired impact to reduce abuse.

70

- **International Collaboration in Research**: Collaboration between countries and international organizations in research can help share knowledge and best practices. Research initiatives at the global level can provide a more complete view of the problem and encourage the implementation of evidence-based solutions.

Global Statistics on Psychological and Verbal Abuse

The National Survey on Violence Against Women in the United States (NVAW, 2000) revealed that more than 50% of women who suffer psychological abuse also report that the aggression is daily or weekly.[10]

Statistics can be a powerful tool to illustrate the magnitude of the problem and raise awareness. Here are some key figures:

- **Global Prevalence**: According to the World Health Organization (WHO), approximately one in three women worldwide has experienced physical or sexual violence by an intimate partner at some point in their lives. Although the focus is usually on physical violence, psychological and verbal abuse is equally prevalent and can coexist with other forms of violence.

- **Impact on Mental Health**: Multiple studies have found that women who experience psychological and verbal abuse have a significantly higher risk of developing mental disorders, such as depression and anxiety, some highlighting women exposed to emotional abuse are more than twice as likely to suffer from mental health problems compared to those who have not been abused.

- **Economic Impact**: Psychological and verbal abuse also have an economic impact. Gender-based violence, including psychological violence, costs economies billions of dollars a year in terms of lost productivity, healthcare costs, and support services.

- **Intergenerational Effects**: Research has shown that children who grow up in homes where psychological and verbal abuse occurs are at a higher risk of replicating this behavior in their own adult relationships, perpetuating an intergenerational cycle of violence.

Challenges in Identifying Psychological and Verbal Abuse

Identifying psychological and verbal abuse can be challenging, both for victims and for the professionals trying to help. The insidious nature of this type of abuse means that it is often hidden in plain sight, and the signs can be difficult to spot even for those close to the victim.

- **Normalization of Abusive Behavior**: Many times, victims do not recognize that they are being abused because they have internalized the behavior as normal or deserved. This normalization process can be a result of manipulation and gaslighting, where the abuser distorts reality to make the victim doubt their own judgments and perceptions.

- **Stigma and Shame**: The social stigma associated with being a victim of abuse, especially psychological and verbal abuse, can prevent people from seeking help. Shame and fear can lead victims to remain silent, perpetuating the cycle of abuse.
- **Lack of Awareness**: Many people, including health and wellness professionals, may not be trained enough to identify psychological and verbal abuse. This can lead to signs of abuse being overlooked or minimized, leaving victims without the support they need.
- **Difficulty Proving Abuse**: Unlike physical abuse, which can leave visible evidence, psychological and verbal abuse is more difficult to prove. The lack of tangible "evidence" can complicate victims' efforts to seek justice or legal protection.
- **Cycle of Abuse and Reconciliation**: The cycle of abuse, which includes a reconciliation or "honeymoon" phase, can confuse victims and make them believe that the abuse is not that severe or that their partner will change. This cycle perpetuates

hope that the abuser will reform, which can prevent the victim from seeking help.

The Role of Society and Culture in Psychological and Verbal Abuse

Cultural and social norms play an important role in perpetuating psychological and verbal abuse. Understanding these influences can help develop more effective strategies to address and prevent abuse.

- **Gender Norms and Machismo**: In many cultures, traditional gender norms that reinforce machismo and women's sub-ordination contribute to psychological and verbal abuse. These norms can justify control and domination in relationships, and delegitimize victims' grievances, perpet-uating an environment in which abuse is tolerated or even expected.
- **Family Roles**: In some societies, women are expected to assume subordinate roles within the family, which can facilitate abuse. The emphasis on obedience and sacrifice

for the family's well-being can make women feel guilty for speaking out against abuse or seeking outside help.

- **Stigmatization of Divorce and Separation**: In cultures where divorce or separation is highly stigmatized, victims may feel trapped in abusive relationships for fear of social disapproval or religious condemnation. This stigma can hinders victims from leaving abusive relationships.

- **Media Representations**: The media can contribute to the normalization of psychological and verbal abuse by glorifying toxic relationships or presenting abusive behaviors as romantic or passionate. These distorted representations can influence perceptions of what constitutes a "normal" relationship and cause victims to tolerate unacceptable behavior.

- **Lack of Resources in Marginalized Communities**: Marginalized communities, including those with low incomes, ethnic minorities, and LGBTQ+ people, often face additional barriers to accessing support resources. Discrimination, poverty, and a lack of culturally competent services can leave victims in these communities especially vulnerable to abuse.

Resources for Victims of Psychological and Verbal Abuse

The path out of an abusive relationship is complicated and challenging, but there are resources and strategies that can be vital for victims. These resources can help victims regain their autonomy, heal emotionally, and build a future free of abuse.

Psychological Support and Therapy

- **Individual Therapy**: The support of a psychologist or therapist specialized in domestic violence is essential. Individual therapy can help the victim process the trauma, identify patterns of abuse, and develop strategies to regain self-esteem and autonomy. In many cases, Cognitive Behavioral Therapy (CBT) is used to help victims restructure negative thoughts and learn new ways to cope.

- **Support Groups**: Participating in support groups can be a valuable experience for victims. These groups, often led by mental health professionals, offer a safe space to share experiences, receive emotional support, and learn from others. Knowing that they are not alone in their struggle can be a great relief for victims, and groups can provide a network of support and solidarity.
- **Helplines**: Many organizations offer phone lines or online chats to provide immediate support to victims. These lines are often staffed by trained professionals who can offer real-time advice, referrals to local resources, and help planning a safe exit. In many countries, these helplines are available 24/7.

Legal Resources

- **Protective Orders**: In many countries, victims of abuse can apply for protective orders or injunctions that prohibit the abuser from approaching them or their children. These orders may include measures such as no contact, expulsion of the abuser from the shared home, and restrictions from approaching certain places, such as the victim's work or school.

- **Legal Counsel**: Access to a domestic violence attorney is crucial for victims. An attorney can provide guidance on legal rights, help the victim file complaints, and represent them in court proceedings. Additionally, in cases of severe abuse, the attorney can assist in pursuing criminal justice against the abuser.
- **Shelter Services**: Shelters for victims of domestic violence offer a safe and confidential place where victims can escape abuse. These shelters typically provide temporary housing, counseling, and support services to help victims rebuild their lives. Some shelters also offer legal services and assistance for reintegration into society.

Social and Financial Assistance

- **Financial Aid Programs**: Many victims of abuse remain in toxic relationships due to economic dependence. Government and nongovernment programs can offer financial assistance, such as grants, food stamps, and housing assistance. These programs are designed to provide crucial financial support as victims begin to rebuild their lives outside of the abuser's control.

- **Training and Employment**: Economic independence is a key factor in a victim's ability to break the cycle of abuse. Government organizations and agencies offer job training programs and job search assistance to help victims gain the skills needed to find a job and maintain their financial independence.

- **Housing Programs**: Finding a safe place to live is a primary concern for victims who leave an abusive relationship. There are emergency and long-term housing pro-grams that provide safe housing for victims and their children. These programs often include additional support, such as, job search help and counseling.

Community Support Networks

- **Non-Governmental Organizations (NGOs):** There are numerous NGOs dedicated to providing support to victims of domestic violence. These organizations offer a range of services, from legal advice and support to temporary housing and training programs. NGOs also play a crucial role in advocating for public policies that protect victims and promote gender equality.[11]
- **Religious or Spiritual Support:** Some victims find comfort and support in their religious or spiritual community. Religious leaders can provide moral and emotional guidance, and many congregations offer specific support programs for victims of abuse. However, it is important that these leaders are trained to handle abuse cases in ways that prioritize the safety and well-being of the victim.

- **Women's Solidarity Networks**: Women's groups in the community often act as informal support networks, offering advice, companionship, and practical assistance to victims. These networks can be a valuable resource, especially in areas where formal resources are limited. Solidarity among women can help create a sense of belonging and empowerment, crucial for victims' recovery.

Difficulty Breaking the Cycle

- **The Cycle of Hope and Reconciliation**: Many victims find themselves trapped in a cycle in which the abuser alternates between violent behavior and promises of change. During the reconciliation phase, the abuser may promise to improve and appeal to the idea of keeping the family together. The victim, wishing to believe that the situation will improve, may cling to the hope that the abuser will change, making the decision to leave the relationship even more difficult.

- **Internalization of Responsibility**: The pressure to maintain family unity can lead victims to internalize responsibility for the success or failure of the relationship. They may feel guilty about the abuse they suffer and believe that it is their duty to fix the situation. This distorted perception reinforces the abuser's power dynamic and makes the victim feel even more trapped.

Overcome the Pressure

- **Education and Empowerment**: It is crucial that victims of abuse receive education about the dynamics of abuse and the importance of their individual well-being. Understanding that the responsibility for violence lies solely with the abuser, not with them, is an essential first step in breaking the cycle of abuse.
- **Legal and Community Support**: Having legal advice and the support of community organizations can provide victims with the necessary tools to face social and family pressure. These resources can help victims

make informed decisions and build a support network that supports them during and after they leave the abusive relationship.

- **Redefining the Concept of Family**: It is important for victims and society in general to understand that a healthy family is not one that simply stays together, but one in which all its members live in an environment of respect, love, and security. Separating from an abuser does not mean destroying a family but protecting it and giving it a chance to heal and thrive.

Conclusion

Psychological and verbal abuse is a serious form of abuse that requires a deep understanding for effective intervention and support. By recognizing the characteristics, impacts, and mechanisms of these abuses, better help and prevention can be provided for those affected. Awareness and education are essential to combat this problem and support victims in their recovery process.

Understanding the cycle of abuse and its impact on victims is essential to addressing and overcoming the dynamics of abuse. Breaking the cycle requires courage, support, and a clear strategy. Through education, self-help, and professional support, it is possible to regain control and build a life free of abuse.

Part III: Other Testimonies

Shannon

I moved to a spa town in northern Chile, where my new partner lived. During a walk on the beach, my daughter befriended another little girl, which led me to approach the mother. I saw despair and sadness on her face, something that perhaps other people would not have seen if they had not experienced the same thing. I perceived this only from the expression in her eyes.

At first, we talked only about trivialities: our children and current events. I think she noticed something special about me, maybe that I paid attention to her and listened to her. After a while, I told her part of my story. She looked at me very surprised. I was about to cry, but she reassured me and said she perfectly understood, and I was blessed to have been able to escape. This went deep into my heart and I thanked her. "I, on the other hand, am trapped," she said, and burst into tears. Now I was the one who consoled her and encouraged her to tell me about her experience.

Shannon was a young woman, but she looked aged. Her hair unkempt and matted, and generally washed out, with a lost distant demeanor. She told me about when she met Jose, while spending time with mutual friends, they fell in love immediately. They went out dancing and dining several times. Jose, being an important and wealthy man, showered her with gifts, trips, and compliments. He was very charming, polite, and a gentleman. He seemed to be the perfect man.

They married a few months later, and soon she began to notice the change in him. He demeaned and humiliated her in front of friends and forbade her from working after they had their first child, according to him, so she could devote more time to the baby. She agreed, thinking perhaps that way he would be calmer and not act violently. However, over time, the negativity increased.

Previously, Shannon had been a successful professional, manager of a major company, and now she didn't feel capable of anything. Her self-esteem had dropped too low, and fear had risen so much that she was on the verge of suicide. I explained to her as best I could the situation she was in and advised her to leave her abuser. However, she told me it was impossible, as he was very powerful. She was convinced she had no chance of escaping. I suggested for her to at least try to put him in his place when he abused her verbally or psychologically, but she just looked at me resignedly and invited me to her apartment which was nearby. I was just recovering myself and was unsure how to best help her. I felt very frustrated

Once in the apartment, I realized the magnitude of the desolation in which this man had things. From the outer appearance, it was a gated and luxurious condominium, however, the inside was desolate. It barely had furniture, only what was strictly necessary, with almost no ornament or decoration to provide family warmth. It was dark and cold, with opaque curtains and colors. The girls played while we had tea and cookies and tried to forget, at least for a while, about our pain.

Unfortunately, I could not continue to see Shannon because I moved to another place further south. I was discouraged and felt very helpless because I was not able to make her understand that the power to change her situation was in her. I wanted to empower her to be courageous and determined to find a way out of the clutches of her abuser. I wasn't prepared to help as much as I wanted to. Hopefully, I gave her some light, and a glimpse of future possibility.

My Mother

Sadly, I realized my own mother was in a relationship with a misogynist, but he was much more charming, since he belonged to the artistic environment, and his abuse was carried out in a very disguised way, almost unrecognizable to others. The violent episodes occurred when he came home drunk late at night, making a tremendous fuss and threatening to kill my mother.

On more than one occasion, I called a good friend of my mother's, who arrived with the police, but nothing happened because my mother did not press charges out of fear, and that was it.

I remember begging this man for my mother's life on my knees, as he threatened her with a knife. Thank God, I managed to calm him down and get him to go to sleep in his drunkenness. Fortunately, for my family, that man fell in love with a neighbor and, after nineteen years of marriage to my mother, they separated without too much negative attention, even though he was guilty of deception and adultery for more than three years.

My mother came to live with me and my small family to protect herself in case he tried to hurt her again, which thankfully did not happen. Years later, he died.

Vicky

Vicky's case was dramatic and, at the same time, inspiring. She was twenty-five years old when she met Ralph, the one who she thought was the love of her life. Although she noticed he had some vices such as liquor and marijuana, she reasoned she could help him by giving him a lot of love and understanding. Soon they began to live together and, although they had not planned it, she became pregnant, and they had a beautiful baby boy. When the baby was five months old, she discovered he was unfaithful to her and, although in great pain, she asked him to go live somewhere else.

Vicky was devastated and also suffered from postpartum depression. Fortunately, she had the support of her mother, close friends, and other women from a program she participated in for mothers with newborn children, which helped her to a great extent, overcome this bitter moment. Vicky was empowered to move on and fight for her baby.

After sharing custody of the baby with her ex Ralph for a while, Vicky realized he was not a good role model to their son and decided to move out of the country.

Soon after, Vicky met another man who offered her safety, support, and affection, or so she thought. This man convinced her to go to the United States, where her son, was born. Vicky agreed, not imagining it would be the beginning of another great disappointment.

A few months after arriving in the United States, Vicky and her new love, Carlos, got married. At the time, she thought he was sincere in his love, but all he wanted was for her to help him with residency in the country, since Vicky is an American. Almost immediately the escalating arguments and mistreatment began, not only towards her, but also towards her son.

Vicky began to feel more and more belittled, disregarded, and unhappy, especially because, although she didn't know for sure, she sensed her little boy was being abused, which made her feel very guilty. Vicky knew my previous story, so she recognized the abuse and began planning how to get out of the relationship.

One day, when the situation became untenable, Vicky went to her mother. However, her mother was unable to receive her because she lived with a cousin who, fearing COVID and retaliation from Carlos, did not allow Vicky and her son to live with them.

With no other options, Vicky had to find a way to survive in her home with Carlos. Vicky distanced herself from Carlos and told him to sleep in her son's room, away from her, and if he dared to harm her or her son, she would report him and stop the residency process. Carlos calmed down, but from that moment on, Vicky had to live several months in great fear and humiliation.

Finally, after several months of much pain, Vicky's mother bought a mobile home, and Vicky and her son were able to move in with her, which was a tremendous relief.

Vicky was later told by a mechanic friend of the family's, that Carlos had visited him in the past to talk about a vehicle. They talked for over an hour, then the mechanic accompanied him to his car. To the mechanic's surprise, he saw Vicky's son in the car and rebuked Carlos for having left a minor alone in a car for so long. This could have been a catastrophe, but fortunately her son was fine, and asked if he could get out of the vehicle.

As Vicky shared her story with me, she cried out of helplessness, anger, and sadness, realizing she made the right decision to leave such an abusive man. From that moment on, she promised to take much more care of her little one and herself, since she was overweight and completely neglected in her physical appearance and health. I advised her to take things slowly, to recover and truly heal from everything she experienced before she entered another love relationship, otherwise, she would attract more of the same.

Tina

Tina and I met while working together in customer service. It was a fast paced and hectic work environment. Whenever we could we got together during lunch and talked. After a few weeks we began to have much more trust in each other and our conversations became more personal.

The subject of abuse came up and I told her my story with Mark. Every time we talked about the subject, I noticed she paid closer attention to me. One day she told me she wanted to know more since it was very similar to what she was living at that time. Knowing I had an opportunity to help her, I went more in depth. I shared in detail what I had lived, what I had learned through research, and what I experienced throughout the whole healing process.

She then decided to tell me her story. She allowed me to include her in this book, hoping it will help many women realize what they are experiencing, what it is called, how to respond, and safely get out of and stay clear of abusive relationships. Here is Tina's story, in her own words:

My Life with Calvin

At first everything was going very well, and Calvin seemed like a good man. Things happened to formalize the relationship, and we got married. I was head over heels in love with Calvin and I was also happy because I knew through marriage, I would obtain legal immigration status in the United States of America.

I have always considered myself a free, independent, and very intelligent woman in all aspects of my life.

<u>April 2018</u>
Living my first year as an immigrant in the United States in the state of Florida, I downloaded a dating app. I basically only met and talked to one guy; his name was Calvin. From that moment we started to get to know each other by chat and days later we had our first date.

We went to dinner at a restaurant where we could get to know each other a little more. Calvin, a North American who only spoke English, and I, a Colombian just learning English. Calvin made a wonderful first impression. He appeared to be a tender man, a little shy, he didn't quite understand me, but he tried hard to. He looked very patient and kind and intentionally put forth effort to make me feel good.

After dating for more than three months, I was forced to make a decision, either to return to my country-of-origin Colombia, or find a host family who would serve as a sponsor, so I could remain in the United States.

I knew of a potential host family in another state. Calvin, saddened and not wanting me to leave, offered to marry me. I reasoned it out before deciding. Even if we lived together and started a family, there was the option of divorce if it didn't work out, and I wanted to end things.

It took me a couple of weeks to finalize what direction to go. After a few talks with my mom we concluded that Calvin was a wonderful man and nothing could go wrong, so getting married was the best option.

We had a very private wedding, just the two of us. We hoped to later have a big wedding in Colombia with our families. His family was in the US, but lived in the far northern states, so it was a distance to travel. Although his father lived with him, he did not accompany us that day.

The plan was for me to move in with Calvin, Calvin's dad, and his new wife, who was a Chinese woman and spoke absolutely no English. They also apparently had a very private wedding.

Days before I moved in, we went out to a bar with a friend who was visiting us. Everything was fine at first until Calvin drank a few beers and the effects of the alcohol kicked in. My friend met a Mexican guy that night who invited us all to an after party. Being young, in our early twenties, excited to explore a new country, my friend and I were looking forward to going, along with Calvin. We left the bar and without warning, Calvin disappeared in the streets of downtown Melbourne. A few minutes later we found him walking alone, a little lost and very angry. He wanted my friend and I to go home and was rude to the new Mexican friend we had just made, who not wanting any trouble, decided to say goodbye to us and left.

Calvin made us chase him at a very fast pace for several blocks because he was the one who drove the car that night. He did nothing but scold me and ridicule us about the "American dream", making fun of the fact that we would never find it. We finally made it to the car. Calvin and I dropped my friend off at her house and went back to Calvin's.

After two hours of arguing in his room, I still didn't understand exactly what he wanted from me. I just wanted to rest and go to sleep, but he went on and on about my supposed "American dream" mixed in with other offensive words.

A few days later, the time came for me to officially move into his house. I was very happy. For the most part, Calvin treated me well and we had a close connection. I was looking forward to starting our new life together.

For many months, I was unable able to work because the law did not allow me to do so until I received my work permit. In the meantime, I dedicated myself to improving my English and taking courses related to my professional career of industrial engineering. He came home from work elated to see me there, almost always with a well-prepared lunch, being a woman totally available to him.

After only three weeks of living together, his arrivals began to be a little stormy. His countenance changed. He barely greeted me or even turned to look at me. At first, I wanted to believe it was the stress of work.

I did not know *that* would be my life with him. A man with fewer and fewer words to say, who completely ignored my existence. My self-esteem and happiness fell to the ground.

I talked to my mom often and our conversations filled me with life. I didn't let her know what was going on with Calvin. My English improved a lot, and I was doing well in my online courses. I started exercising so that depression would not overtake me.

Calvin's cooking skills were very basic, and he depended on me to prepare his meals. Every time we went to the grocery store, he behaved in a very cruel and selfish way. I am used to being an independent woman, but at this time of my life, I was completely dependent on Calvin, and he used that to take advantage of me and humiliate me. He made me fully aware it was his money being spent. He would always walk in front of me as if we were not together and say things like, "Do we need anything from this aisle? No? Well then, let's go!", without giving me the opportunity to even answer his questions. We simply got what was needed for his preferred meals and nothing I particularly liked.

When it came to having sex, initially we did very well. Shortly after living together as husband and wife, our sex life drastically declined. It was solely to meet his physical needs, at the time and place of his choice. I was often woken out of my sleet at two or three in the morning, so he could satisfy himself. He did not care that he was cutting into my sleep hours or even if it was something I wanted. Calvin was a selfish man in bed.

Finally, I received my papers to be able to work and travel. I found a job at a call center. I was able to make a few friends there, but I could never accept their invitations to get together outside of work because of Calvin. He considered that to be disrespectful. He said things like, "A *good* wife doesn't do that. A *good* wife stays at home taking care of her husband." It was his very sexist comments and views that inhibited me from my freedom.

As time went by, our relationship deteriorated more and more.

Tina got to the point where she could not continue. By now, my daughter was older, and we worked together to get Tina out of Calvin's house. We were ready to call the police if he became violent with her or us. When we showed up, Calvin was surprised to see us and let her go without any problem.

I stayed outside while my daughter went in the house to help Tina get her things. Tina's terrible living conditions were revealed. There was just a mattress on the floor to sleep on and a few other pieces of furniture. The kitchen was almost empty. The entire place was dark and moist.

Tina stayed with us for a short time and then went back to her country. She is doing well. She travels with her friends, works wherever she likes, and lives free and independently. Thankfully, she was able to safely get away from her abuser and moved forward with her life. We keep in touch with her, and she is our eternal friend.

Part IV: Alternatives & Practical Advice

The misogynist will have won if he leaves his wife out of control. In general, men, to a greater or lesser extent, can sometimes try to dominate by disqualifying a woman or making her feel guilty when the fault has been his.

It is here that women must claim their position without resorting to violence or abuse. It is important to be assertive and help uncover misconceptions.

Knowing how to recover lost ground is essential.

It's crucial that women don't confuse standing up for themselves with yelling or begging. These reactions are often ineffective.

When a woman does not firmly establish her boundaries and advocate for herself, she leaves the misogynist total control over the relationship. The woman may seem out of control, whether she screams, begs or cries, and the misogynist will have won if he manages to destabilize her emotionally.

Many professionals agree, there are common reactions to a partner's abuse that are ineffective, such as:

- Apologizing
- Begging
- Crying
- Arguing
- Defending oneself
- Accusing
- Shouting
- Threatening

Beyond these ineffective responses, there are really effective strategies many women have simply never learned to use. Before implementing your response, decide which aspects of the relationship need to change.

When a misogynist has already defined what *you* should or should not think, feel, or behave, imposing a monopoly on what is right in the relationship, not considering your feelings and needs, practice incorporating these phrases in your vocabulary to advocate for yourself:

- "This is what I think."
- "This is what I believe."
- "This is what I'm going to do."
- "This is what I won't do."
- "This is what I want."

Next, make a list of the things *you* want within the relationship:

- I want equality in terms of money.
- May my sexual needs be as important as yours.
- I want to have a say in the decisions that concern us.
- I want respect for the work I do, whether it's outside or inside the home, or both.

- I want to participate in activities that are important to me, not just the ones you choose.

Add personal aspects:

- I want to work (if you don't).
- I want to perfect my career.
- I want more help at home.
- I want more help with the kids.

Set things you'll never allow again:

- I won't allow him to yell at me.
- I won't allow him to insult me.
- I won't allow him to criticize me.
- I won't allow him to diminish me.
- I won't allow him to control me and tell me what to do.
- I won't allow him to humiliate me.

REMEMBER, WE *ALL* HAVE RIGHTS.

Decrease the use of phrases, such as:

- "I'm sorry."
- "Is this okay?"

- "Do you agree with me?"
- "Do you like it?"
- "If you're going to get angry, I'll do whatever you want."

People who feel good about themselves are able to say, "I can give you my opinion, and let you decide whether you like it or not." In a good relationship, two opinions can coexist. Now you need to decide what you really want, for example:

- I want respect.
- I want to be able to express myself.
- I want to be heard.
- I want to be valued.
- I want to be taken seriously.
- I want tenderness.
- I want understanding.
- I want the right to have my own beliefs and opinions.

If you want these things and are in a misogynistic relationship, you need to take action for your mental, emotional, and spiritual health, which are in serious danger of being severely affected.

Psychological and verbal abuse can be devastating, and it is essential for victims not only to acknowledge the abuse but also adopt effective strategies to protect themselves and regain control. Here are alternatives and practical tips that may be helpful to those facing these situations.

Strategies for Claiming Personal Standing

The goal is not simply to "win" an argument, but to restore respect and fairness in the relationship. Here are ways to do it:

- **Stay Calm and in Control**: Calm and self-control are essential. Emotional reactions such as screaming or crying can be misinterpreted or manipulated. Instead, respond firmly and calmly so that your messages are heard clearly.
- **Set Clear Boundaries**: Clearly define and communicate what your boundaries are. Use clear and direct statements such as: "I

will not tolerate you talking to me in that way," or, "I will not accept that my opinion is dismissed."

- **Use Affirmative Phrases**: Shift your focus to affirmations of your rights and desires. For example, "I need respect in our communication," or, "It's important to me for our decisions to be made together."

Alternative Strategies to Ineffective Behaviors

Dr. Susan Howard highlights behaviors that are often ineffective in handling abuse. Instead, consider more effective strategies:

- **Avoid Emotional Retouching**: Instead of apologizing or begging, focus on maintaining a constructive and assertive dialogue. Apologies and pleas can be perceived as an admission of guilt or weakness.
- **Develop Assertiveness**: Practice assertiveness by expressing your needs and desires without aggression. Assertiveness is based on clear and respectful comm-

unication, and it can help establish a balance in the relationship.

- **Seek Professional Support**: Considering the help of a therapist or counselor can be crucial to developing effective communication skills and strategies for managing abuse.

Rights and Self-Esteem in the Relationship

The affirmation of personal rights is essential for an equitable and respectful relationship:

- **Right to Respect and Valuation**: Make sure that your basic rights, such as respect and consideration, are recognized and maintained in the relationship. This includes being heard, valued, and taken seriously.
- **Mental and Emotional Health Care**: Prioritize your emotional and mental well-being. If a relationship is harming your health, consider seeking professional help and exploring alternatives to protect your well-being.

- **Act Purposefully**: If you are in an abusive relationship, take steps to protect your mental and emotional health. This may include setting clear boundaries, seeking outside support, and considering separation if necessary for your safety and well-being.

Resources and Support

- **Seek Support Groups**: Participating in support groups for victims of abuse can provide a network of understanding and help. These groups can offer practical advice, emotional support, and additional resources.
- **Consult Specialists:** Therapists, counselors, and abuse attorneys can offer personalized guidance and assistance to manage the situation effectively.
- **Research Community Resources**: Many communities offer resources such as helplines, shelters, and legal services to support people in abusive situations.

Strategies for Regaining Personal Control

Regaining control over your life is essential to your well-being. Here are additional strategies to bolster your autonomy:

- **Develop Assertive Communication Skills**: Assertive communication involves expressing your thoughts and feelings clearly and respectfully. Practice saying what you need without blaming or attacking. For example, "I feel uncomfortable when you talk to me that way. I'd rather we talk respectfully."

- **Create a Personal Action Plan**: Make a plan that includes concrete steps to improve your situation. This can include short and long-term goals, such as seeking professional support, improving your self-esteem, or developing new skills.

- **Foster Financial Autonomy**: Financial independence can be crucial to having control in an abusive relationship. Consider exploring opportunities to improve your financial literacy, look for a job, or increase your income.

Facing the Cycle of Abuse

Breaking the cycle of abuse requires a careful and well-thought-out strategy. Here are some additional steps:

- **Documenting Incidents of Abuse**: Keeping a detailed record of incidents of abuse can be helpful in identifying patterns and providing evidence if you decide to seek legal help.
- **Establish a Support Network**: Make sure you have friends, family, or support groups you can trust. This network can offer emotional and practical support, and be a valuable resource in times of need.
- **Have an Emergency Plan**: In case the situation worsens, it is important to have a safe exit plan. This can include having money set aside, knowing where to go in case of an emergency, and having copies of important documents.

Strategies to Strengthen Self-Esteem

Self-esteem is the perception and valuation that a person has of themselves. In the context of an abusive relationship, it can be severely affected. Strengthening self-esteem is crucial to regain personal control and well-being. Here are detailed strategies for improving and strengthening self-esteem:

- **Participate in Activities You Enjoy**: Engaging in activities that bring you personal satisfaction and joy can help strengthen your self-esteem and provide a sense of accomplishment.
- **Practice Self-Care**: Take time to take care of yourself physically, emotionally, and mentally. This includes getting enough sleep, eating well, and engaging in activities that relax you.
- **Develop New Skills**: Learning new skills or improving existing ones can boost your self-confidence and ability to meet challenges.

Identifying and Challenging Negative Beliefs

- **Recognize Negative Beliefs**: Identify negative beliefs you have about yourself, such as, "I'm not good enough," or, "I don't deserve respect." These beliefs are often the result of manipulation and abuse.
- **Challenge Limiting Beliefs**: Question the validity of these beliefs. Ask yourself if there is concrete evidence to support them and if they are actually true. It may be helpful to write down a list of evidence that contradicts these beliefs.
- **Replace with Positive Affirmations**: Replace negative beliefs with positive, realistic affirmations. For example, if you used to think, "I'm not able to make decisions," change it to, "I have the ability to make informed and effective decisions."

Goal Setting and Achievement

- **Define Clear and Achievable Goals**: Set specific and achievable goals in different areas of your life, such as professional, personal, or educational. Break down big goals into smaller, more manageable steps.

- **Celebrate Achievements**: Recognize and celebrate your successes, regardless of their size. Celebrating achievements, no matter how small, can help build a positive perception of yourself.
- **Keep a Record of Achievements**: Keep a journal of accomplishments and successes. Reviewing this record can serve as a tangible reminder of your abilities and accomplishments, especially in times of doubt.

Develop Emotional Resilience

- **Practice Self-Empathy**: Be kind to yourself and recognize that it's normal to have difficult times. Practice self-empathy by offering support and understanding to yourself rather than self-criticism.
- **Learn Stress Management Techniques**: Develop stress management skills, such as meditation, yoga, or breathing techniques. Reducing stress can help improve your emotional state and self-esteem.

- **Seek Professional Counseling**: Considering working with a therapist or counselor can provide additional support in addressing self-esteem issues and learning effective strategies for recovery.

Promote Healthy Relationships

Fostering healthy relationships is key to your well-being:

- **Encourage Open Communication**: In any relationship, clear and open communication is critical. Practice expressing your thoughts and feelings honestly and responsively.
- **Set Clear Expectations**: Make sure that both you and your partner understand and respect the expectations in the relationship. This includes discussing and agreeing on how conflicts should be handled and how each other's needs and desires should be addressed.
- **Seek Equitable Relationships**: In a healthy relationship, both partners should feel that they have an equal voice and

respect. Avoid relationships where one member has disproportionate control over the other.

Support and Education Resources

Ongoing education about the abuse and the resources available can be vital to your recovery:

- **Rights and Resource Education**: Learn about your rights as a victim of abuse and the resources available in your community. This includes knowing local laws, support services, and organizations able to offer assistance.
- **Workshops and Seminars**: Attend workshops and seminars on abuse and self-esteem can provide additional tools and strategies for managing and overcoming abuse.
- **Specialized Professionals**: Connect with therapists, counselors, and abuse attorneys who offer personalized support and guidance to help you make informed and effective decisions.

Final Thoughts

I wish with all my heart that this book illuminates the path to liberation, transformation and happiness in your life, at the same time that it gives you the courage to leave the networks of abuse to build your well-being with your children, other family members, and support network. You are very valuable, you just have to find *that* value in your heart, a great fraternal embrace to guide you to the light of faith and true Love.

Today in my golden years, I feel proud to have not only survived the abuse, but to have healed and share the relationship I have with my daughters and my mother. With them, I have a very special love and connection, we have in turn an extraordinary trust and mutual support.

My eldest daughter and my youngest daughter have been my light on a difficult and at times dark path, they have been my inspiration and my life force. They have given my existence the courage to move forward despite the challenges. My grandchildren are my joy and the hope for a better tomorrow every day.

My mother, who I thank God for still having with me, has been my unconditional support and an essential guide in this adventure of living.

I am blessed and grateful in life for having known how to draw lessons from my adversities and break family patterns, so they are no longer repeated through generations but turned into allies that serve me to improve my present and therefore my future.

I invite you, if you are living in a toxic relationship of abuse, to take all precautions and build a better future for yourself and your children, full of blessings, joy, hope, and much prosperity. A big hug that fills your heart with strength to always do the best for you and yours, thousands of blessings, and may life bring you abundance in health, money, and love.

About the Author

Julia Manriquez

was born in Colombia and grew up in Chile.
She began writing at a very young age.

Julia worked as a Physical Education teacher
in Chile and continues her career in
education, now working in Florida as a
Bilingual Assistant, holding a degree in
English as a Second Language.

She enthusiastically researches and
practices alternative medicines and therapies,
promoting a wholistic approach
to life and wellness.

Julia is a proud mother of two adult daughters
and joyful grandmother of two grandchildren.

Recommended Books & Websites for Additional Support

American Psychological Association
https://www.apa.org/

Economic Commission for Latin America
and the Caribbean (ECLAC)
https://www.cepal.org/en

European Union Agency for Fundamental Rights
https://fra.europa.eu/en

National Center on Domestic and Sexual Violence
https://www.ncdsv.org/

National Coalition Against Domestic Violence
https://ncadv.org/

National Domestic Violence Hotline
https://www.thehotline.org/

National Institute of Mental Health
https://www.nimh.nih.gov/

Office of Justice Programs
Full Report of the Prevalence, Incidence,
and Consequences of Violence Against Women
https://www.ojp.gov/pdffiles1/nij/183781.pdf

United Nations
https://www.un.org/en/

United Nations Population Fund
UNFPA is the United Nations
Sexual and Reproductive Health Agency.
https://www.unfpa.org/

U.S. Centers for Disease Control and Prevention
https://www.cdc.gov/

World Health Organization
https://www.who.int/

Endnotes:

Part I: My Testimony

1. "Misogynist." Merriam-Webster.com Dictionary, Merriam-Webster, https://www.merriam-webster.com/dictionary/misogynist. Accessed 21 May. 2025.

Part II: Understanding the Root of Abuse

1. Forward, Susan; Torres, Joan. *Men Who Hate Women and the Women Who Love Them: When Loving Hurts and You Don't Know Why*, (Random House Publishing Group, 2011), pages 99-120.
2. Ibid., 33, page 8.
3. mha2975. "Mental Abuse vs. Emotional Abuse." Mental Health Answers, 19 Sept. 2023, mentalhealthanswers.org/mental-abuse-vs-emotional-abuse/.
4. Gordon, Sherri. "What Are the Signs of Verbal Abuse?" Verywell Mind, Verywell Mind, 20 May 2024, www.verywellmind.com/how-to-recognize-verbal-abuse-bullying-4154087.
5. APA Div. 12 (Society of Clinical Psychology). "What Is Cognitive Behavior Therapy?" American Psychological Association, American Psychological Association, 2017, www.apa.org/ptsd-guideline/patients-and-families/cognitive-behavioral.
6. "Abusive Relationships (for Teens) | Nemours Kidshealth." Edited by Allison T. Dovi, KidsHealth, The Nemours Foundation, Aug. 2021, kidshealth.org/en/teens/abuse.html.
7. Participation, Expert. "Domestic Abuse Act 2021." Legislation.Gov.Uk, Statute Law Database, 2021, www.legislation.gov.uk/ukpga/2021/17/contents.
8. "Eye Movement Desensitization and Reprocessing (EMDR) Therapy." American Psychological Association, American Psychological Association, 2017, www.apa.org/ptsd-guideline/treatments/eye-movement-reprocessing.
9. United Nations General Assembly resolution 34/180. "Convention on the Elimination of All Forms of Discrimination against Women New York, 18 December 1979 | Ohchr." United Nations Human Rights Office of the Higher Commissioner, 3 Sept. 1981, www.ohchr.org/en/instruments-mechanisms/instruments/convention-elimination-all-forms-discrimination-against-women.

10. Michele C. Black; Kathleen C. Basile; Matthew J. Breiding; Sharon G. Smith; Mikel L. Walters; Melissa T. Merrick; Jieru Chen; Mark R. Stevens, "The National Intimate Partner & Sexual Violence Survey (NISVS): 2010 Summary Report." National Coalition Against Domestic Violence, 2010. Higher Commissioner, 3 Sept. 1981, www.ohchr.org/en/instruments-mechanisms/instruments/convention-elimination-all-forms-discriminat ion-against-women.
11. "Non-Governmental Organizations (NGOs) in the United States." U.S. Department of State, U.S. Department of State, 20 Jan. 2025, www.state.gov/bureau-of-democracy-human-rights-and-labor/releases/ 2025/01/non-governmental-organizations-ngos-in-the-united-states.

www.ingramcontent.com/pod-product-compliance
Lightning Source LLC
Chambersburg PA
CBHW071007120626
46546CB00003B/972